MANAGING ORGANIZATIONAL CHANGE

Leading Your Team Through Transition

Cynthia D. Scott, Ph.D., M.P.H.
and
Dennis T. Jaffe, Ph.D.

CRISP PUBLICATIONS, INC.
Los Altos, California

MANAGING ORGANIZATIONAL CHANGE
Leading A Team Through Transition

Cynthia D. Scott, Ph.D., M.P.H. and
Dennis T. Jaffe, Ph.D.

CREDITS
Editor: **Michael Crisp**
Designer: **Carol Harris**
Typesetting: **Interface Studio**
Cover Design: **Carol Harris**
Artwork: **Ralph Mapson**

Copyright © 1989 by Crisp Publications, Inc.
Printed in the United States of America

Crisp books are distributed in Canada by Reid Publishing, Ltd., P.O. Box 7267, Oakville, Ontario, Canada L6J 6L6.

In Australia by Career Builders, P.O. Box 1051 Springwood, Brisbane, Queensland, Australia 4127.

And in New Zealand by Career Builders, P.O. Box 571, Manurewa, New Zealand.

Library of Congress Catalog Card Number 88-63805
Scott, Cynthia and Jaffe, Dennis
Managing Organizational Change
ISBN 0-931961-80-7

PREFACE

> *The present is a time of great entrepreneurial ferment, where old and staid institutions suddenly have to become very limber.*
>
> —*Peter Drucker*

Organizational Change has become a way of life. Mergers, takeovers, layoffs, deregulation, downsizing, new technology, and increased competition are daily occurrences. As a manager and leader you are challenged to maintain performance under chaotic conditions. Your workforce can be confused, resistant and disheartened. Job security, company loyalty, and steady career development are no longer available as rewards for performance. What can you do to build a motivated and productive work force under these conditions?

The skills and strategies in this book will help you to:
- Understand your role in the changing workplace
- Explore what the future workplace will be like
- Lead organizational culture change
- Understand and manage people through change
- Provide change leadership
- Use organizational events to manage transition
- Deal with individual and group resistance
- Negotiate new work arrangements
- Spot common errors
- Prepare your group for change
- Become a change master

This book will give you the step-by-step advice and activities to become an effective **Change Leader** in your organization.

Good Luck!

Cynthia D. Scott, Ph.D., M.P.H.   Dennis T. Jaffe, Ph.D.

ABOUT THIS BOOK

MANAGING ORGANIZATIONAL CHANGE is not like most books. It stands out from other books in an important way. It's not a book to read—it's a book to *use*. The unique "self-paced" format of this book and the many worksheets encourage a reader to get involved and try some new ideas immediately.

This book will introduce the critical building blocks of how to successfully lead your team through change. Using the simple yet sound techniques presented can make a dramatic change in your ability to help those you manage handle the traumas of change as positively as possible.

MANAGING ORGANIZATIONAL CHANGE (and the other titles listed in the back of this book) can be used effectively in a number of ways. Here are some possibilities:

—Individual Study. Because the book is self-instructional, all that is needed is a quiet place, some time and a pencil. By completing the activities and exercises, a reader should not only receive valuable feedback, but also practical steps for self-improvements.

—Workshops and Seminars. The book is ideal for assigned reading prior to a workshop or seminar. With the basics in hand, the quality of the participation will improve and more time can be spent on concept extentions and applications during the program. The book is also effective when it is distributed at the beginning of a session, and participants "work through" the contents.

—Remote Location Training. Books can be sent to those not able to attend "home office" training sessions.

There are several other possibilities that depend on the objectives, program or ideas of the user. One thing for sure, even after it has been read, this book will be looked at—and thought about—again and again.

CONTENTS

Managing Organizational Change is based on two interactive workshop programs: *Mastering Change* and *Managing The Human Side Of Change*. These workshops have been developed in conjunction with Flora|Elkind Associates, a leading training and development firm. The programs have been implemented at major corporations all across the country to help thousands of managers and employees learn the skills they need to manage change.

For more information on how you can use these workshop programs to help your organization, please call:

Flora|Elkind Associates
1388 Sutter Street, Suite 610
San Francisco, CA 94109
(415) 776-6676

INTRODUCTION

GETTING THE MOST FROM THIS BOOK

Working with managers and leaders in organizations, the authors have found that the process of organizational change is often scary and confusing. Yet there has been only slight focus by most organizations on the management of human capital through periods of change. A classic book on mergers and acquisitions devotes only four pages on what to do with the people in the organization during periods of change. Many companies have discovered although they have moved the desks, they haven't moved the hearts of the employees who work there. When this happens management is frustrated by resistance and lack of productivity among the workforce. This book provides strategies and skills that will help managers through the wilderness of change.

Each change is unique and requires a specialized approach to ensure positive outcomes. There is no single foolproof list of steps. Depending on the situation, as manager, you must customize and experiment. We invite you to use the **Change Checklist** in this book as a guide when you undertake a change in your organization.

Change management is a new skill. None of us took Change 101 in business school. In that regard, we are all discoverers and inventors with the basics of this book and your common sense and good judgement. You will be able to turn your ideas into positive results when dealing with change.

SECTION I

UNDERSTANDING ORGANIZATIONAL CHANGE

The pace of organizational change is increasing. Recent studies show that:

► Companies expect to cut an average of 15% of their work force.

► The hundred biggest mergers in the U.S. during a recent year affected four and a half million workers.

► In the past five years more than 12,000 U.S. companies and corporate divisions have changed hands.

► 70% of mergers end up as financial failures.

► The take over trend is increasing. It is more than double what it was three years ago.

► Certain industries (such as major brokerage firms) have cut significant percentages of their workforce in recent years.

► U.S. manufacturing needs to increase productivity dramatically to remain competitive with foreign industry.

> *"The adaptive corporation needs a new kind of leadership. It needs 'managers of adaptation' equipped with a whole new set of non-linear skills. Above all the adaptive manager today must be. . .willing to think beyond the thinkable—to reconceptualize products, procedures, programs, and purposes before crisis makes drastic change inescapable.*
>
> *Warned of impending upheveal, most managers still pursue business as usual. Yet business as usual is dangerous in an environment that has become for all practical purposes, permanently convulsive."*
>
> —*Alvin Toffler,* **The Adaptive Corporation**

WHAT CHANGES HAVE YOU EXPERIENCED?

Take a moment to check below any changes you have faced in the last two years:

- ☐ technology changes
- ☐ accelerated product cycles
- ☐ merger
- ☐ acquisition
- ☐ divestiture
- ☐ lay offs
- ☐ downsizing
- ☐ start up of new division or company
- ☐ spin offs
- ☐ top management change
- ☐ culture change—new policies, values, expectations
- ☐ deregulation
- ☐ re-organization
- ☐ serious and new competitors
- ☐ expanded organizational liability

Add your own

- ☐ _____
- ☐ _____
- ☐ _____

"WE'VE JUST BEEN DOWNSIZED"

WORKPLACE 2000—REMEMBERING THE FUTURE

In the 1960s the definition of management competence rested on specific management planning, scheduling, and controlling techniques. Today, competence is based more on attitudes, approaches, philosophies, values, and the ability to create improvements in health, innovation, and productivity. A manager today plays on a different field, and must manage in a different way. He or she must be a **change manager,** or, as this book recommends, a **change leader.**

Change leadership is not a skill reserved just for top management. As organizations struggle to respond to the pressures of competition (including the global business environment), you and your work team have to learn to move quickly to attain higher standards and increased productivity. Is this possible? In many organizations it is critical; for if you do not succeed, your organization may not survive.

In recent years many broad changes have taken root in the workplace. While the specifics may vary, change is happening in more workplaces and at a faster rate. The reasons are not just "fashion." The new strategies are all premised on the fact that organizations today need to be organized for constant change. The structures, motivators and pressures within an organization during change are very different from the traditional process. Modern organizations ask each individual to take more responsibility and put a premium on more collaborate work teams. Even the structure of some organizations becomes flatter and less hierarchical.

SUCCESSFUL ORGANIZATIONS ARE NOT DEAF, MUTE OR BLIND ABOUT THE FUTURE

LOOKING TOWARD THE YEAR 2000

Looking toward the year 2000, the following are some of the elements you can expect to see in most organizations. Check any you have already noticed in your organization.

I have observed:

☐ more employee involvement in all levels of decision making

☐ increased emphasis on "meaningful work"

☐ more responsibility for individual employees

☐ fewer managers and more participation in the form of self-managing teams

☐ a movement toward profit sharing or employee ownership

☐ a focus on human capital as demonstrated by an investment in training, re-training, and new skill development

☐ an atmosphere that encourages more mutual respect and trust

☐ an increase in the protection of employee rights

☐ programs that support balancing work and family

☐ increased encouragement of learning and creativity away from the workplace via tuition and fee reimbursement plans

☐ better recognition and reward for superior performance

☐ smaller managerial groups

☐ greater diversity in the workforce with more women and minorities

☐ a continuing need for workers with specialized skills

(Add others you have noticed)

☐ _____

☐ _____

☐ _____

☐ _____

☐ _____

LEARNING HOW TO LEARN

In a constantly changing organization, no set of skills stays useful forever. The technical skills a person learns in school, or on the job, quickly become obsolete.

Not long ago a clerical person had to know how to insert and align carbon paper while typing a document. Today that same person must understand computers, fax machines and the concept of electronic mail.

Today, it is more important for workers **not to know** a particular set of skills; but to understand **how to learn.** To be successful, people today have to master how to learn a wide range of new skills quickly. They have to be open to changing old ways of doing things in order to learn new tasks and adapt on new skills. Most can't stay narrowly specialized, they must become generalists.

What does this mean? First, that every employee will have to take greater responsibility. In the authors' best selling recent book **Take This Job and Love It,*** this is called the **two-job concept.** In addition to handling a particular job, the ''second job'' for an employee is to help his or her organization change and continuously improve.

Second, it is no longer possible for a company to guarantee an employee a specific job. If a person wants to remain with an organization, he or she will have to learn to master many jobs and continuously expect to shift. In many cases this will be not just in one department or specialty, but broadly, from manufacturing to marketing, or from technical engineering to sales. The most valuable employees will be the ones with the flexibility to master the most challenges.

Third, organizations will have to be reorganized into a less hierarchical structure and become more participatory. Work groups will be given more authority to decide how they will accomplish tasks. Information will have to be broadly shared, because more groups will need it. As a manager, your role will shift away from the traditional role of controlling and move toward keeping your team trained and flexible in order to accomplish continually changing goals.

---

*Take This Job and Love It, Simon & Schuster, New York, 1988.

ORGANIZATIONAL RESPONSES TO CHANGE

Change creates pressure in any organization. This is especially true when the organization has not had much experience dealing with change. The first taste of major change in this situation can be traumatic. Many organizations today are struggling to adjust to the new environment of rapid change.

In many organizations there are different responses to change among the different levels. This is shown and explained below:

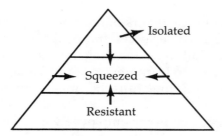

Top Management:

In a traditional company, top management has a hard time coming to grips with the direct implications of the change. They often underestimate the impact that change has on their employees. They tend to isolate themselves. Often they engage in strategic planning sessions and gather information in survey reports. They avoid communicating or seeking ''bad news,'' because it is difficult for them to admit they ''don't know.'' They expect employees to ''go along'' when a change is announced and blame their middle managers if people resist or complain about the change. They often feel betrayed when employees don't respond positively.

Middle Management:

Managers in the middle feel the pressure to ''make the organization change'' according to the wishes of top management. They feel pulled in different directions. Middle managers often lack information and leadership direction to focus on multiple priorities. They are caught in the middle, and often fragmented because they don't have clear instructions. They feel besieged with upset, resistant or withdrawn employees who no longer respond to previous management approaches, and deserted, blamed or misunderstood by their superiors.

Employees/Workers/Associates:

Workers often feel attacked and betrayed by changes announced by management. They are often caught off guard, not really believing that ''my company could do this to me''. Many respond with resistance, anger, frustration, and confusion. Their response can solidify into a wall of ''retirement on the job''. They become afraid to take risks, be innovative, or try new things. They experience a loss of traditional relationships, familiar structure, and predictable career advancement patterns.

THE ROLE OF THE MANAGER/LEADER DURING CHANGE

In times of change each manager, supervisor, and team leader will be called upon to lead change in his or her group. Top management should not be expected to manage the transition of individual work groups. Many middle managers wait for their leaders to tell them what to do. In many cases communication between top executives and middle managers is poor and there is no strategy to effectively announce and implement the change.

Managers want answers. When there are no ready solutions they often blame top management for leaving them in the dark. The best advice for these managers is to stop waiting and become a leader of their team. If they sit around waiting, the wave of change may wash over them and drown them. To stay afloat they must learn to manage change. Change offers both uncertainity *and* opportunity for them as a manager. How they manage themselves and their work group will make all of the difference. By following the steps and strategies in this book they can learn how to view change as an opportunity and create a climate of productivity and growth.

This book was developed to assist you to lead your group to respond effectively to change. Changes can affect your organizational culture—the basics of how you do things-your products, customers, management practices, leadership styles, etc. Those who know how to react in this environment will be the winners.

Helping yourself through change is an important part of being a change leader. *Managing Personal Change** by the authors of this book focuses on the skills needed to complete a personal transition successfully.

Going through any major change will challenge the way we view ourselves. Major changes can be like the death and rebirth of a company. Living through this process is similar to a major remodeling of a kitchen. To obtain the final result you want, you first must rip out the old kitchen, leaving a lot of basic structure and emptiness. Then you begin to bring in new cabinets and appliances so they fit coherently. Once you add the final touches you can move back in and feel comfortable and productive again. It always takes longer than you thought and costs more than you estimated.

*Managing Personal Change, Crisp 1989. To order, use the form in the back of this book.

FANTASIES ABOUT CHANGE

Organizational transition is slow, expensive and difficult. There is a tendency to believe that change can be instant, painless, and quick. Managers often seem to expect that changes they make will:

1) Not be disruptive.
2) Not cost much and be quick to implement.
3) Solve previous organizational problems.

These myths may help you understand why many organizations do such a poor job managing the process of change, or become reluctant to accept the challenge of other changes, if previous attempts have gone badly.

The process of making a major change to an organization's culture requires people to let go of "how it was" and move through a period of doubt and uncertainty. When you are managing this process it becomes all-consuming and must be managed sensitively. Organizations that handle the process of changing an organization's culture well, reduce the time required for similar changes in the future.

CHANGING A CULTURE

Change is often nothing more than a simple shift of technology, or some reporting relationships. But when major change hits a company, or a severe crisis demands a response, what really is changing is the "corporate culture." The way the organization has been doing things. This much change demands a major shift in the way in which the work gets done. It is no longer possible to remain a caretaker, set in your ways. Rather, the challenge is often to increase productivity, while moving a work group in a new direction. This book is about that challenge.

CHANGE CAN BE FRIGHTENING

BASIC GUIDELINES DURING CHANGE

Following are nine guidelines for changing a corporate, or team, culture. They will be presented more fully in later sections of this book. Whenever possible, you should:

1 Have a good reason for making the change

Culture changes are usually not fun. Take them seriously. Make sure you understand why you are making the change and that it is necessary.

2 Involve people in the change

People who are involved are less likely to resist. Being a part of the planning and transition process gives people a sense of control. Ask for opinions about how they would do it. Consider conducting surveys, focus groups, and polls.

3 Put a respected person in charge of the process

Each change needs a leader. Select someone who is seen in a positive light by the group.

4 Create transition management teams

You need a cross-section of your group, to plan, anticipate, troubleshoot, coordinate and focus the change efforts.

5 Provide training in new values and behavior

People need guidance in understanding what the ''new way'' consists of and why it is more desirable. Training brings groups together. It allows them to express their concerns and reinforce newly learned skills.

6 Bring in outsider help

For some reason, there is often more power in what an outsider says than the same suggestions coming from inside. Use this power to reinforce the direction you want to go.

7 Establish symbols of change

Encourage the development of newsletters, new logos or slogans, and/or recognition events to help celebrate and reflect the change.

8 Acknowledge and reward people

As change begins to work, take time to recognize and recall the achievements of the people who made it happen. Acknowledge the struggle and sacrifices people have made.

REVIEW OF SECTION I

You cannot escape or hide from organizational change. It comes with the territory. Problems come when people are not allowed to manage the change, and are not taught the skills to learn how to learn. In order for an organization to adapt to change, it needs to help its people move through change.

SECTION II

PREPARING FOR CHANGE

What is my first step?
Who needs to be involved?

I'm a great believer in luck, and I find the harder I work the more I have of it.
Thomas Jefferson

PREPARING FOR CHANGE

Key Elements of Change Management

Top management sometimes plans extensively for strategic changes in an organization, but places very little emphasis on how to handle the transsition from the old way to the new way. When this occurs, often the new goal, system, organization or project is simply presented as a direction or decision to a work team. When the team has not been consulted, it comes as a shock. The change is announced and implementation is left up to the group. When this happens to you, as the manager involved, you are on the spot. You need to produce results but can only produce when your team is fully behind the changes. Top management too often considers implementation of the change a footnote of their plan. Your work team may consider the same change as a crisis of the first magnitude.

Most organizational difficulty with change manifests itself in this transition period. This is where people get stuck. People become confused, anxious, angry, and often unproductive. Your job as manager is to move your team through change in the smoothest way possible, regardless of how well or poorly the change was addressed.

Gaining Control by Giving It Up

Following is a major lesson in leadership. It simply is that you can't move through change *and* keep previous levels of tight control over your people. The lesson is that you can gain control over change by giving it up.

In effective organizations, people share basic goals and communicate clearly, directly and regularly about what they are doing. Each person goes about his or her work with greater flexibility than is common in less effective organizations. If you manage an effective organization, during change, you will benefit by exercising a new type of leadership. Less as a controller and more as a coordinator, focuser and facilitator. Only you and the group together can make things happen. This takes place when you learn how to intelligently delegate some of your control to your team.

As manager you have special responsibilities to maintain strong upward lines of communication. If you keep the information you receive from above to yourself, or feel you are the only one who knows how to handle change, your controlling leadership will not be helpful in implementing the changes. Your group will not learn, will not have the information they need to make shifts, and will not feel they share in the change unless you involve them by giving up some of your control.

PREPARING FOR CHANGE (Continued)

Power and Influence

Most of the major organizational changes you will experience in your career will not be initiated by you. You may be able to anticipate change or see it coming, (for example, the need for new technology), however, most of the time you will be handed change as a fact. When this happens, a common reaction, regardless of level is an attitude of helplessness. ''What can I do?'' or ''Has anyone taken us into account,'' can lead to inactivity and frustration. When this happens, workers spend their time bemoaning the change, dreaming of the old days, or criticizing the judgment of top management.

Your task as change agent is to shift the energy away from the feeling of being powerless and the feeling of security from the past, toward seeing the opportunities of the future. You can do this by calling attention to the ways your team can make a difference.

Here is how to begin.

Think about a recent change that has been announced in your organization. Then, in the worksheet on the following page fill in which aspects of the change are ''**Givens**'' in the space provided. Usually these are beyond your control. They could include aspects of timing, personnel, budget or other factors.

Next, write those aspects of the change that you and your team can **Control** in the space provided. This is where you need to really dig. Some things may seem to be givens but may be somewhat under your control.

Finally, think about what aspects of the change you and your team can **Influence** and write them as indicated. Remember, you can always communicate or negotiate with other groups in your organization. Your group can initiate communication and discussion with any other group. What aspects of the change do you need to talk about, need better clarification, or need to present new information about? How can you accomplish this?

Taking control and exerting influence are crucial aspects of change management. By the end of this book, you'll regard almost everything about a change as negotiable. Top management doesn't automatically consider everything. If your team has better information, or sees things differently, you owe it to your organization to negotiate and discuss it.

Use the exercise on the following page for yourself when you are preparing for a change. Repeat it with your team to help them plan their response to change. You will learn that your team will see things differently from you, just as you often see things differently from your superiors.

CONTROLLING CHANGE

In the space provided, think about a recent change in your organization and describe which aspects of that change were ''givens'', which were ''negotiables'' and which were ''controllable'' in the space provided:

GIVENS—ASPECTS OF THE CHANGE I(WE) HAVE NO CONTROL OVER:

NEGOTIABLES—ASPECTS OF THE CHANGE THAT WE CAN INFLUENCE OR DISCUSS WITH OTHER GROUPS:

CONTROLLABLE—ASPECTS OF THE CHANGE MY TEAM CAN CONTROL:

PLANNING FOR CHANGE

The following steps will help you successfully introduce and implement a change in your group. You and your team will need to do your homework to complete each stage. Depending on circumstances, you may not go through each stage in perfect order, but at least you should be aware of them. Otherwise you risk having you and your group not being adequately prepared for implementing the change successfully.

I   Preparation: Anticipating key elements.

II   Planning: Getting people together to plan the response.

III Transition Structures: Establishing special ways of working together, and temporary organizational structures.

IV   Implementation: Activating a flexible response and learning cycle.

V   Reward: Acknowledging the people who made it work.

Each step will be carefully considered in the following pages.

THE BETTER YOU PLAN, THE "LUCKIER"
YOU WILL BE WHEN IMPLEMENTING CHANGE

I PREPARATION:

Before the change, whenever possible, follow these five steps:

1. ☐ Prepare your employees.

Let them know what is happening ahead of time. Telling them too far ahead of time is not always better (for example telling people 8 months before a change only leaves time for anxiety to build up.)

2. ☐ Describe the change as completely as you can.

How do you see the change affecting individual employees and the work group as a whole? Identify who will be most affected and approach them first.

3. ☐ Research what happened during the last change.

Does your group have a positive history of their ability to manage change or was the last change traumatic? Learn from past experience and let this background influence your current actions.

4. ☐ Assess the organizational readiness of your team.

Are they ready to undertake a change? An organization or group that isn't mentally and emotionally prepared will tend to stay in denial, rather than accept the change and move on.

5. ☐ Don't make additional changes that aren't critical.

People need all the stability they can get during change. Don't change the payroll dates, the working hours or cafeteria procedures when you are making large scale organizational changes. Change the most important things, one at a time.

II   PLANNING:

Think it through. During this stage:

1. ☐ **Make contingency plans.**

Think of options to the proposed change: If things go one way, what will you do...? What about the other way...? Anticipate the unforseen, the unexpected and any setbacks.

2. ☐ **Allow for the impact of change on personal performance and productivity.**

Don't expect people to get up to speed in an instant. It will frustrate whatever sense of achievement they are experiencing.

3. ☐ **Encourage employee input.**

Discuss each stage of the way and ask for suggestions.

4. ☐ **Anticipate the skills and knowledge that will be needed to master the change.**

Do your people have them? Have you prepared training plans?

5. ☐ **Set a time table and objectives so you can measure your progress.**

THINK IT THROUGH!

III TRANSITION STRUCTURES:

Special activities for a special time. After Step II planning:

1. ☐ **Create a transition management group to oversee the change.** Develop temporary lines of authority. This group is responsible for taking the pulse of the group and helping identify possible roadblocks.

2. ☐ **Develop temporary policies and procedures during the change. Demonstrate flexibility to try new things. Loosen control and procedures.**

3. ☐ **Create new communication channels.** Remind people why the change makes sense. Use hot lines, electronic mailboxes, newsletters, video tapes, general meetings, training sessions, posters, etc., so people will receive information fast. The cost of gossip is high, forestall it though clear, accurate communication.

4. ☐ **Meet frequently to monitor the unforseen to give feedback, or to check on what is happening.** Make feedback a daily event.

ESTABLISH TEMPORARY STRUCTURES FOR SUCCESS

IV   IMPLEMENTATION:

Take clear, flexible action to accomplish this:

1. ☐ **Provide appropriate training in new skills and coaching in new values and behaviors.**

2. ☐ **Encourage self-management.** Inform each person he or she is accountable for some aspect of the change.

3. ☐ **Give more feedback than usual to insure people always know where they stand.**

4. ☐ **Allow for resistance.** Help people let go of the "old". Prepare to help those having special difficulty making the adjustment.

5. ☐ **Give people a chance to step back and take a look at what is going on.** Keep asking, "is the change working the way we want it to?"

6. ☐ **Encourage people to think and act creatively.**

7. ☐ **Look for any "opportunity" created by the change.**

8. ☐ **Allow for withdrawal and return of people who are temporarily resistant.** Don't cross off people as irretrievable.

9. ☐ **Collaborate.** Build bridges from your work group to other work groups. Look for opportunities to interface your activities.

10. ☐ **Monitor the change process.** Conduct surveys to find out how employees are responding to the change.

V   REWARD:

Sharing the gains:

1. ☐ **Create incentives for special effort.** Celebrate those who lead the change. Give one-time bonuses to groups who have come through the change smoothly.

2. ☐ **Celebrate by creating public displays that acknowledge groups and individuals who have helped make things happen.**

REVIEW OF SECTION II

You may not know when a change is in the works, but when it happens you are far from helpless. While there may be much beyond your control, many aspects of implementing change can be anticipated and influenced. Begin change management by seeking new options, and planning. Involve your group during change as soon as possible.

SECTION III

WHAT HAPPENS TO PEOPLE?

"Some people learn from their experiences, others never recover"
"People do not fear change, they fear loss"

Things fall apart. The center will not hold
W. B. Yeats

UNDERSTANDING LOSS

Change occurs when something ends and something new or different starts. The period between these two points is *transition*. This is where people have to learn to let go of the old and embrace the new. Usually it means moving from the familiar to the unknown. Even when change is positive, this psychological process affects us. Most of us have a strong response to any change. One of the strongest can be a feeling of loss, along with the struggle to accept a new direction. Change can produce physical symptoms such as sweating, sleep loss, and/or emotional distress which will affect the quality of work.

The most common error in managing change is underestimating the effect it has on people. Many managers think that if they just tell their employees to change, they will. They do not realize how upsetting it is to give up work patterns that are familiar. Always remember how much will be disrupted and understand that people need time to adjust.

Even when change is positive—promotion, expansion, going public, new markets, etc.—it is not uncommon for a person to feel an ending or loss associated with it. Managers often have a hard time understanding the loss associated with change. If you don't manage loss, you can't lead people in a new direction.

Types of Loss

When a major shift or change occurs within an organization, employees normally experience several types of loss including the loss of:

1. Security—Employees no longer feel in control or know what the future holds, or where they stand in the organization.

2. Competence—Workers no longer feel like they know what to do or how to manage. People sometimes become embarrassed when they are faced with new tasks because they don't know how to do them. It is hard to admit you don't know how to do something.

3. Relationships—Here the familiar contact with people like old customers, co-workers or managers can disappear. People often lose their sense of belonging to a team, a group, or an organization.

4. Sense of Direction—Employees lose an understanding of where they are going and why they are going there. Meaning and mission often become unclear.

5. Territory—There is an uncertain feeling about the area that used to belong to them. This can be work space or job assignments. Territory includes psychological space as well as physical space.

UNDERSTANDING LOSS (Continued)

Each of the losses described on the preceding page has a cost. Any type of loss, even of a work space or familiar technology, can trigger an emotional response that resembles grief. You must help your employees move past their loss, to accept and move forward in the new direction.

It is important to understand that people are not weak or old-fashioned if they experience loss caused by change. This is a normal part of transition. In fact, people who do not display any feeling of loss often save it up and become overcome by a seemingly small transition. It is healthier to express and acknowledge loss when it occurs, so those involved can move through the transition process more quickly. One job of the manager is to acknowledge that a loss has occurred, not pretend it is business as usual. Unacknowledged loss will usually lead to resistance and disruption down the road.

IT IS NORMAL TO FEAR THE UNKNOWN

HOW PEOPLE CHANGE

People change from being led; not from being told.

A common fantasy is that if you order people to change, they will. This belief often leads managers to behave like drill sergeants—ordering employees around. Usually, the response to this approach will be resistance, defensiveness and/or withdrawal.

People do not normally change their behavior simply from information. For example, how many people have quit smoking because of the written warning on the cigarette package?

It is far more common for *people to change because of the support, encouragement, caring confrontation, and empathy* of a relationship. Becoming a leader and forming a supportive relationship is often a new skill for managers who have taken a more traditional approach to management. The more involved you are with your team, and the more involved they are with each other, the easier change will be. Creating trusting relationships requires skill and can put a manager in a more exposed situation. However, managers who can create supportive relationships are more successful during periods of change because their team will trust and follow them.

Incentives and rewards

Because most change is resisted it is important to create incentives for those who adapt to change professionally and thoroughly. To become a change agent you might:

• Create public recognition of the change masters.

• Reward those who remove roadblocks to change.

• Give a special one-time bonus to those acquiring the new skills and/or behaviors that make the change work.

• Incorporate good ideas and new suggestions from team members as a regular part of your meetings.

MOVING FROM DANGER TO OPPORTUNITY

Change often involves elements of both danger and opportunity. When people approach a change, their first response might be to see it as a threat or a danger. When this happens, they fear and resist the change.

Once the change occurs, it is not uncommon for those effected to begin getting used to it. Often, during this period, people begin to see that the change may lead to new opportunities. Some see that the new way may indeed be more effective and offer the potential for new freedom and power. Once people accept that a change can provide new opportunities and possibilities, the change is well on the way to successful implementation.

> **Think of a recent change you experienced and write your reactions in the space provided:**

• How was this change experienced by you as a threat or danger?

• What hidden opportunities or possibilities did you find in the change?

THE PHASES OF TRANSITION THROUGH CHANGE

Danger and **Opportunity** can be further subdivided into the two phases shown below. These provide a model of four phases people commonly go through when facing change.

- **Danger** can be subdivided into:
  Denial
  and
  Resistance

- **Opportunity** can be subdivided into:
  Exploration
  and
  Commitment

Most people move through these four phases in every transition. However, some may go quickly or get bogged down in different phases. Effective leadership can help a group, and each of its members, move through the phases from denial to commitment.

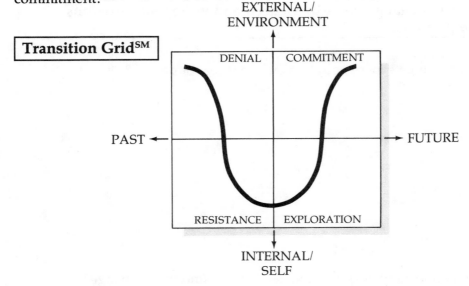

Changes in your organization will transport your team through the four phases of the transition process shown above. Think of this process as descending into a valley and then climbing back out. The transition leads from the way things were done in the past toward the future. During change, people focus on the past, and **deny** the change. Next, everyone goes through a period of preoccupation, wondering where they stand and how they will be affected. This is normally where **resistance** occurs. As they enter the **exploration** and **commitment** phases they start to look toward the future and the opportunities it can bring.

---

*The Transition Grid^SM is part of the Change Programs, Managing the Human Side of Change & Mastering Change, offered by Flora|Elkind Associates in San Francisco and is used with permission.

DIFFERENT STAGES CALL FOR DIFFERENT STRATEGIES

Different stages call for different strategies. During change you will probably have employees in different stages. You will need to be situational in your application of techniques to help your people through the change. The checklist below can help you diagnose which stage employees are in. Also, it is not uncommon to find an employee swinging between two stages. When this happens, use the strategy described in this section at the earliest stage until that person is ready to move forward.

WHAT DO YOU SEE IN YOUR WORK GROUP?

During a recent change in your organization, check any behavior that you observed within your work unit:

Denial
- ☐ it will be over real soon
- ☐ apathy
- ☐ numbness

Commitment
- ☐ teamwork
- ☐ satisfaction
- ☐ clear focus and plan

Resistance
- ☐ can't sleep at night
- ☐ anger/fights
- ☐ gave my all and now look what I get
- ☐ withdrawal from the team

Exploration
- ☐ overpreparation
- ☐ frustration
- ☐ too many new ideas
- ☐ have too much to do
- ☐ can't focus

DENIAL:
THE FIRST REACTION TO CHANGE

When a big change is announced, the first response is often numbness. The announcement doesn't seem to sink in. Nothing happens. People continue to work as usual. It appears that productivity will continue and nothing will be affected.

The stage of **Denial** can be prolonged if employees are not encouraged to register their reaction, or if management acts like employees should just move directly into the new ways. Denial is harmful because it impedes the natural progression of healing from a loss (i.e. the old way of doing things) to moving forward. Employees stay focused on the way things were (neglecting both themselves and their future), not exploring how they can or need to change.

Because people are often blind to problems during the denial phase, a manager can mistakenly think he or she has jumped directly to the final phase of Commitment. This hope can be reinforced by motivational speakers who simplistically encourage people to think positively, pull themselves up by their bootstraps and move on to excellence. This is called a **Tarzan Swing**[SM] and appears to work for a short while, (usually until some indicator shows that productivity is decreasing). At this point an organization often calls a consultant to "fix" problems, like stress, that the employees are experiencing. The focus on the individual, rather than on the organization's response to the change, leaves an important side of change management untouched.

Top management is particularly prone to want a **Tarzan Swing**[SM] in their organization from the initial announcement of change. They often don't see why people should have trouble. They seem to believe that people are being paid to put aside their feelings, or they may feel that the company simply doesn't have time to move through the other stages. But wishing doesn't change the sequence; it just drives it underground. The next section of this book provides strategies to move a team through the denial stage.

RESISTANCE: PHASE TWO

Resistance occurs when people have moved through the numbness of denial and begin to experience self-doubt, anger, depression, anxiety, frustration, fear or uncertainty because of the change. Elizabeth Kubler-Ross identified this stage in conjunction with her work with the dying. Some types of organizational change are similar to a death experience. If a company is sold, merged or there are layoffs, the expectations, hopes, promises and actual work goes through something close to a death for certain employees. People focus on the personal impact of the change on them.

In the resistance phase, productivity dips drastically and people are often upset and negative. Managers hear lots of grumbling, the personnel department will be extra busy and the copy machines will be churning out resumés. Accidents, sickness and work related absences multiply. Outside programs on change management are most often requested during the Resistance phase.

While it is difficult for a company to openly experience negative expressions, that is exactly what helps minimize its impact. Allowing people to express their feelings and share their experience makes this phase pass faster. People who believe they are the only one who ''felt'' a certain way, or think their reactions are more intense than their colleagues feel better when they learn through sharing that others feel the same.

Closed cultures where these responses cannot be shared will prolong this phase. Expressing feelings is what helps employees change. During the resistance period organizations can make effective use of organizational rituals (ie. picnics, parties, awards, luncheons, etc.) to address these normal responses. People need a way to say good-bye to the old and begin to welcome the new. Strategies for dealing with resistance will be covered later in this book.

Eventually everyone reaches a low point and begins to move up the other side of the change curve. This shift, clearly felt, but different for everyone, indicates things are getting better. Work groups suddenly notice a renewed interest in work and feel creativity coming back. This signals that phase two is passing.

EXPLORATION AND COMMITMENT: THE FINAL PHASES

During the **Exploration** phase, energy is released, as people focus their attention on the future and toward the external environment once again. Another word for this phase is "chaos." As people try to figure out new responsibilities, search for new ways to relate to each other, learn more about their future and wonder how the new company organization will work, many things are in question. There is uncertainty during this phase, including stress among those who need a lot of structure. During exploration people tend to draw on their internal creative energy to figure out ways to capitalize on the future. This phase can be exciting and exhilarating. It can create powerful new bonds in a work group. Section VII of this book will spend more time discussing visioning and exploration.

After searching, testing, experimenting, and exploring a new form begins to emerge. When this happens, the individual or group is ready for **Commitment.** During this phase employees are ready to focus on a plan. They are willing to re-create their mission and build action plans to make it work. They are prepared to learn new ways to work together, and have re-negotiated roles and expectations. The values and actions needed to commit to a new phase of productivity are in place. This is a phase of where employees are willing to solidly identify with a set of goals and be clear about how to reach them. This phase will last until a new cycle of transition begins with another major change.

Since change is inevitable, a good question might be: will we always be riding on this wave of transition? The ideal answer is yes. For without change we and our organizations would become stale and unresponsive. The challenge is learning to move through the transition as easily and creatively as possible. What helps people navigate through unknown territory is a map of what they can expect and information on ways to respond most effectively to the predictable challenges that are presented.

MANAGEMENT STRATEGIES FOR EACH PHASE

At any point during the change process, your team will probably not be in one phase, but shifting back and forth between phases. As a manager, you need to know what phase your general group is in, as well as that which phase each individual is experiencing. To help your team move through the curve toward commitment, some examples are listed below of what you will observe in each phase. This will help you diagnose where team members stand.

How to Diagnose Each Phase

DENIAL

It is common to observe: withdrawal, ''business as usual,'' focus on the past. There is activity but not much gets done.

RESISTANCE

You will see: anger, blame, anxiety, depression, and even retirement on the job, ''what's the difference, this company doesn't care any more.''

EXPLORATION

You will recognize: overpreparation, confusion, chaos, energy. ''Let's try this and this and what about this . . .'' Lots of energy and new ideas but a lack of focus.

COMMITMENT

Occurs when employees begin working together. There is cooperation, and a better focus. ''How can we work on this.'' Those who are committed are looking for the next challenge.

THE GOAL IS COMMITMENT

MANAGEMENT OF EACH PHASE

What Actions to Take During Each Phase

—DURING DENIAL

Confront individuals with information. Let them know that the change will happen. Explain what to expect and suggest actions they can take to adjust to the change. Give them time to let things sink in, and then schedule a planning session to talk things over.

—DURING RESISTANCE

Listen, acknowledge feelings, respond empathetically, encourage support. Don't try to talk people out of their feelings, or tell them to change or pull together. If you accept their response, they will continue to tell you how they are feeling. This will help you respond to some of their concerns.

—DURING EXPLORATION

Focus on priorities and provide any needed training. Follow-up on projects underway. Set short-term goals. Conduct brainstorming, visioning and planning sessions.

—DURING COMMITMENT

Set long term goals. Concentrate on team building. Create a mission statement. Validate and reward those responding to the change. Look ahead.

Where is Your Group?

Think about how your work group would respond to change during each phase. Make some notes:

During Denial—I believe my group would react by:

_____

During Resistance—I believe the behavior of my group would be:

_____

During Exploration—I feel my group would:

_____

During Commitment—My group would probably:

_____

DURING AN ACTUAL CHANGE SITUATION

List a few key people in your group and, based on the indicators mentioned on the previous page, make a guess where each member is:

NAME	SIGNS OBSERVED	PHASE

1. _____

2. _____

3. _____

4. _____

5. _____

Next, graph your members on the change grid below. Place their initials approximately where they fall on the curve.

Phases of Transition

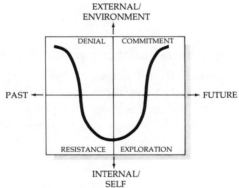

Finally, from your analysis, what approaches do you need to use as a manager to bring your group to the next level?

_____

_____

Who are the leaders, who can help others move along?

_____

_____

Who are stragglers in your group that need special help?

_____

_____

TRAPS

During change, a manager may fall into one of the following traps:

1. Ignoring or resisting resistance.

Resistance is not pleasant to experience. It can feel like everyone is angry at you and you are to blame. This is normally temporary. Denying resistance only makes it go deeper and last longer. Invite it. Seek it out through listening and good communication.

2. Jumping to team building.

When forced with change, many managers think that what they need most is getting people back to working together. When a group is in denial, resistance or the early moments of exploration, you are wasting time to work much in team building. The group needs a chance to complain, assess their loss, before beginning to re-build trust and cooperation.

3. The "Drano" approach—pushing productivity too soon.

Some managers believe that if you demand performance you will get it. Employees may respond in the short run but tend to plateau and actually decrease productivity if their feelings don't match their actions. The danger is that you will end with a "clogged" organization where everything breaks down.

CHANGE MASTERY

The next four sections of this book focus on four competancies that managers need to move their groups successfully through change:

—**Communicating about Change**

—**Dealing with Resistance**

—**Increasing Team Involvement**

—**Visionary Leadership**

SECTION IV

COMMUNICATING ABOUT CHANGE

I must follow the people. Am I not their leader?
Benjamin Disraeli

COMMUNICATING ABOUT CHANGE

Your Role As Manager

As a manager, you are often caught in the middle. You may have a lot, some or virtually no input in a change, yet you have responsibility to make it work in your unit. You have your own feelings about it. At the same time, you are responsible for taking the company position.

The way you bring the message about a change to your team has much to do with the eventual outcome. How you make your announcement, what you say and how you negotiate with your team members will make the difference. Section IV explores methods of announcing change, tells how to monitor responses, and covers negotiating for what needs to be done. The change announcement is most often made during the Denial stage, and sometimes doesn't sink in. When the message is accepted, your group may shift from Denial to Resistance very quickly. You need to learn how to manage these intense responses from your team. This section should help you do just that.

Setting a Climate for Communication

In times of change, maintaining open communication can help prevent rumors, anxiety and mistakes. Often managers avoid delivering unsettling news by claiming they are ''too busy and pressured'' to take time to meet with their people. Studies have shown that if you don't make time early on in the process, you will spend more time later cleaning up the problems.

During change, two-way communication is essential. Every issue must be covered. Different communication forms are recommended. Use hotlines, open forums, newsletters, videotapes, fireside chats, informal discussions—whatever works for you. Repeat the message using various methods of communication regularly.

COMMUNICATING ABOUT CHANGE
(Continued)

How Did I Hear?

Let's examine some ways that people learn about change using yourself as an example.

Think about a recent change you experienced at work.

- How did you first hear about change? How were you informed?

_____

_____

_____

- What were the strengths and weaknesses of the way in which you were informed?

_____

_____

_____

- How would you have preferred to be informed? How could the announcement have been improved?

_____

_____

_____

GUIDELINES FOR COMMUNICATING WITH TEAMS ABOUT CHANGE

Following are some tips for informing your group about change. Place a check mark beside those you currently use. Place an ''X'' next to those you intend to use during the next change.

☐ **1. Talk to People in Person.**

A memo or newsletter is not the most effective way to inform people about important changes. Written announcements don't allow people to express their feelings directly. Written documents are often used to avoid dealing with people's responses. In the long run, this can only backfire. Memos and newsletters are good as a follow-up after a one on one meeting, because people can be in denial and have a hard time ''hearing'' information that disturbs their security.

☐ **2. Tell People the Truth.**

The more informed people are, the less anxious they will be. Unanswered questions are fuel for the rumor mill. If you don't know—tell them so. You don't have to know all the answers. A believable leader doesn't know everything, especially in times of change. Solicit questions and try to find answers to the missing information. Schedule another meeting when you learn more and share that information as it becomes available.

☐ **3. Express Your Feelings.**

Don't exclude information about your feelings. People want to know your reactions. They will feel acknowledged and understood and will be more open if your feelings are expressed. When appropriate tell them how the change affects you personally. Self-disclosure from a leader is a very powerful strategy because you often reflect what they are thinking.

Here's an example...

''In light of this new reorganization, I can guess that some of you are experiencing some confusion and worry about how this will affect your job. As a manager in this division I have some of these same feelings, but am confident things will work out for the best. I want to assure you, I'll work to represent our best interests during the transition period.''

COMMUNICATING ABOUT CHANGE
(Continued)

Why is it Important to Talk?

During change it is important for you to meet with your employees both formally and informally. Keeping everyone informed is the overall objective even though the specific purpose of each meeting will vary as you move through the stages of the change process. Here are some specific purposes for meetings:

1. To announce a change.

2. To provide new information and clarification.

3. To give people a supportive place to express their feelings.

4. To involve employees in the planning and implementation of the change.

5. To provide feedback on how things are going.

6. _____

7. _____

One interesting observation is that a meeting where change is announced sometimes reflects a miniature version of the four phases of the transition cycle. First, there can be denial until the announcement is discussed and understood. Then people may express resistance, by questioning, and complaining or second-guessing. Finally, there can be a shift as people begin to question how they will respond to the future with some constructive brainstorming and planning. Finally, the group may tentatively commit to the direction of the change.

Generally, it's best to meet with your whole group if the change affects them all. If some people are more directly affected, you might meet with them individually immediately before the group meeting so you can explain the situation carefully and/or offer support if appropriate. If individuals will be negatively affected, a pre-meeting will give you the opportunity to deal with this.

Why do People Need Discussions?

People who go through change most successfully benefit from:
- Specific reasons for the change
- Accurate information—the truth
- An opportunity and encouragement to ask questions
- Acceptance of the opportunity to express their feelings
- Personal reassurance

COMMUNICATING ABOUT CHANGE
(Continued)

Holding a Change Meeting

A meeting to announce a change is the best way to inform your group. Meetings are also basic tools for planning, implementing and monitoring change. Meetings reinforce the idea that people are a team who can work together to make things happen. Meetings can let everyone know what is happening and offer opportunities for feedback. During change, you should schedule frequent meetings to insure communication is clear and open.

Planning a Change Meeting

Like any important business activity, it is important for you to do your homework before conducting a change meeting. Review the information to be communicated. Write notes to insure all key information is presented. Think about the best way to introduce the change and the most logical way to present the details. Following is a general format for a change meeting. Make sure you are ready to follow these steps:

☐ Review the need for change and how it came about.
☐ Describe the change in detail.
☐ Explain how the change will affect your group.
☐ Ask for questions about the change. Invite participation.
☐ Listen to feelings and respond appropriately.
☐ Share your personal feelings (if appropriate).
☐ Ask for help and support in making the change work.

Listening During Change

One of the most important elements of communication is listening.* People who feel listened to are less resistant and often move through a change more easily. Active listening is the best technique to help individuals understand their feelings and move more quickly to action.

Listening With the Third Ear

Some managers frustrate their teams by spending the whole meeting talking. They are so busy announcing, explaining, exhorting and pursuading they don't leave time for feedback. Perhaps they fear hearing responses. The secret of being a successful change master is not only talking openly and directly, but also listening carefully to what is said—(and sometimes what is not said). Listening will provide you with messages, meanings and feelings that your team experiences.

---

*For an excellent book on this topic, order THE BUSINESS OF LISTENING using the form in the back of this book.

COMMUNICATING ABOUT CHANGE
(Continued)

Steps of Active Listening

In active listening you pay attention not just to the content of what a person is saying, but also the feelings and underlying emotions that lie *behind* what they say. When you listen actively, you hold back your need to persuade. That can come later. In active listening your goal is:

- to help another person express what he or she feels, and/or wants, and
- to show that you want to understand his or her thinking.

Active listening involves the following behaviors. Check those with which you agree:

☐ 1. **Pay attention with your whole body.**

Sit back and focus on the other person. Don't shuffle through papers or fidget. Extend your full attention.

☐ 2. **Make eye contact.**

Listen with your eyes. Focus on what the person says. Observe his or her expression. Try to determine what the face and body say along with his or her message.

☐ 3. **Show interest.**

Occasionally repeat what you heard the person say to verify his or her message (i.e. "Lets see, you're saying that the re-organization will disrupt your career plan.").

☐ 4. **Ask open-ended questions.**

Draw the person out. Often it takes time to express a point, or reveal honest feelings. Open-ended questions require more than a "yes" or "no" answer (i.e. an example would be: "What was your initial reaction to the change?" or "What do you think the impact of the change will be on the group?").

☐ 5. **Listen to the feelings behind the message.**

In addition to what the person is verbalizing, each statement also says something about the person's feelings and attitudes. Try to hear not just the content, but the feelings that lie behind it. If you have a hunch the person is feeling something, check it out by asking a question, such as "Are you feeling angry about the change?".

☐ 6. **Confirm and clarify what you have heard.**

Make sure you received the meaning of the message accurately, by repeating it back to the person. Try to summarize and get the core of the person's message across. If you do that, the other person will normally be more relaxed and more receptive to discussing options.

COMMUNICATING ABOUT CHANGE
(Continued)

Communicating Clearly

During change a manager often assumes that others will understand what to do. Because of increased pressure there is sometimes a tendency to shorten directions or reduce communications. This is bad because more information is needed during change, not less. Every person needs to assess how he or she will relate to the change. Whether it is a new organization, a new task, or a new technology, people will need to learn how to work together differently. You will need to understand how relationships within your unit will change, about what you expect from each other and how you will work together. Sometimes, you may have to do this several times. During change things are always shifting.

KEEP SURPRISES TO A MINIMUM DURING CHANGE

COMMUNICATING ABOUT CHANGE
(Continued)

Getting your message across

Because communication is key to change management it is important for you to make your communication complete and clear.

Following is a four part formula which will help you communicate clearly. It is:

Behavior + Feelings + Effect + What You Want = Clear Communication
---

Let's look at the parts in more detail:

I. Behavior/Situation:

What has happened? What is the change that needs to be responded to?

> *"Since we've started using the new computers, absenteeism has increased significantly. Let's discuss the situation to see if we can discover the reasons."*

II. Feelings:

What are your feelings about the change? Are you confused, hopeful, or upset?

> *"I'm personally a little frustrated about aspects of the change, and want to learn your feelings about it."*

III. Effect:

What effect will the change have on you? The work group? The project?

> *"The effect of the change has been to put us behind schedule for April."*

IV. What You Want to Happen:

What outcome you would like to see? What do you want the other person to do?

> *"What I'd like, is to see if we can figure out what is happening and what we can do about it."*

Sending a Clear Message

Think of the change you're facing. Is there one person you need to inform about a particular response or difficulty you are having? What message(s) do you need to deliver. Write one out below using the formula:

Behavior _____

Feelings _____

Effect _____

What you want _____

COMMUNICATING ABOUT CHANGE
(Continued)

Choosing the best word for your feelings

Feelings are the hardest to communicate because they can pack an emotional punch and sometimes an intense response. Verbalizing your feelings can cause your listener to withdraw, or become defensive. But that doesn't have to happen. Choosing appropriate words can help. It is usually best to select the least dramatic word that still communicates how you feel.

Think of feeling words as being worth different amounts:

- "25 cent words" are very strong. Examples could be: appalled, aghast, disastrous, deceptive, etc. These words should be used with great care.

- "10 cent words" lie in the medium range. Examples include: "concerned, confused, upset, frustrated, etc."

- "5 cent words" are usually best. Examples are: "confused, curious, interested etc. These are the least likely to encourage a defensive reaction.

People from different cultural backgrounds may hear words differently. Check if you have any concerns so you won't startle or offend anyone needlessly.*

Feeling Words

25¢	10¢	5¢
_____	_____	_____
_____	_____	_____
_____	_____	_____
_____	_____	_____

---

*For an excellent book on this subject, order *WORKING TOGETHER* using the form in the back of this book.

SECTION V

DEALING WITH RESISTANCE

The past is gone; the present is full of confusion; and the future scares the hell out of me!

David L. Stein

46

DEALING WITH RESISTANCE

Spotting Signs of Resistance

Resistance is not only a predictable part of change, it is perhaps the most difficult phase to deal with. People resist for good reasons, even though we would rather they didn't.

These reasons include:

- their security is threatened
- the change threatens their sense of competence
- they fear they will fail at new tasks
- they are comfortable with the status quo

Signs of Individual Resistance:

How many have you observed?

☐ Complaints
☐ Errors
☐ Anger
☐ Stubborness
☐ Apathy
☐ Absence due to illness
☐ Withdrawal

Just as individuals signal resistance, so do work groups and organizations.

Signs of Organizational Resistance:

☐ Accidents
☐ Increase in worker's compensation claims
☐ Increased absenteeism
☐ Sabotage
☐ Increase in health care claims
☐ Lowered productivity

What resistance signs have you noticed in your group?

_____

_____

_____

DEALING WITH RESISTANCE (Continued)

Resistance Paradox

Resistance is usually unpleasant for management. It is not easy to endure complaints or suffer blame from your team employees. In contrast, denial looks much easier. Sometimes managers encourage their team to remain in the denial stage because it is easier for them to manage.

On the other hand resistance is a sign your group has left the state of denial and is ready to move through change. Even though it may be misdirected at first, resistance shows that the person's system of self-defense is beginning to take over; an important step in recovering from change.

Your job as a manager is to put on a "Tomato Suit" and allow yourself, (within reason), to receive the slings and arrows of resistance. Remember, you are the on-site symbol of the change. Try not to take employee resistance personally.

Rituals: Saying Good Bye

One of the most successful things a manager can do during change is to help employees say "good good-byes"—so they can say "good hello's" during Exploration and Commitment. A key element of this process involves accepting the discouragement, sadness or grief that employees may be feeling. The amount of these emotions will vary depending on the amount of loss they are experiencing. A "good bye" for an old procedural system will be much less emotional than moving the business to another state.

One way to help your employees through this bumpy time is by using ritual. We're not suggesting tribal ceremonies from primitive groups; there are plenty of 20th century rituals available. The most successful ones are simple ways to publicly acknowledge losses that people are experiencing. Some examples—any gathering that brings everyone together to remember the past, tell stories about it and acknowledge how important it was at the time. The next page contains some examples.

EXAMPLES AHEAD

DEALING WITH RESISTANCE (Continued)

> ### Examples

- A public housing agency, when moving from an old, crumbling building to a new one across town, cut a piece of the old carpet (the symbol of their past), put it up in their new lounge and covered it with momentos from the previous location.

- During a merger, employees assembled a "time capsule" and buried it with old memos, reports etc. As they threw dirt on it, they told stories about the past.

Events like these have a way of springing up spontaneously. Management often makes the mistake of thinking such events are childish or unnecessary. When people are not given an opportunity to grieve, they move forward at a slower pace. In the long run, this holds up productivity and prolongs resistance.

Saying "good bye" is especially important for people left behind in the case of a reorganization, merger or buy-out. The "survivors" often feel guilty, bitter, distrustful, and depressed. Those left behind also need a chance to say goodbye to the people who have gone.

Think of a change you are going through. What kind of event could you initiate to help your people say goodbye in a positive way?

_____

_____

_____

_____

_____

_____

DEALING WITH RESISTANCE (Continued)

The Troubled Employee

Organizational change is hard enough. When it happens along with other personal problems, it may feel like ''the straw that broke the camel's back.'' It is estimated that 10%–15% of the employee population at any given time has a alcohol/drug or other medical/behavioral problem that prevents them from being fully productive. The added stress of change on a person who is barely coping can be devastating.

All the management strategies in the world will not help them.* They need professional assistance. Because personal problems are increased during periods of stress, such as change, you will probably see an increase in troubled behavior during these times. The safest path is to refer any employee needing attention to professional help through your employee medical or Employee Assistance Program (EAP). Contact your personnel or human resources department for more information.

Remember, covering up poor performance simply extends the time the employee will be distressed before getting help. Avoiding a problem is a form of Denial.

SOME EMPLOYEES WILL HIDE THEIR TRUE FEELINGS OR PROBLEMS

---

*For an excellent book dealing with this topic, order *JOB PERFORMANCE & CHEMICAL DEPENDENCY* using the form in the back of this book.

REVIEW OF SECTION V

Before people accept a change, they must deal with their feelings about loss of their old ways. People need time, acceptance and support to let go of the old and move into the new. The work team can create rituals to say good-bye, while some employees need special help to move on.

SECTION VI

INCREASING TEAM INVOLVEMENT

Life is either a daring adventure or nothing.

-Helen Keller

INCREASING TEAM INVOLVEMENT

The primary complaint of managers during organizational change is the difficulty they experience getting their people motivated. Employees in the early phases of change often are unmotivated. They are negative, or disinterested in work that needs to be done. Their attention is elsewhere. Their problem is normally not a lack of motivation, but rather that they are dealing with other issues.

Motivation is often thought of as a series of devices managers use to get people to do things. The implication is that if the "tricks" weren't employed, employees wouldn't want to do the task.

Newer thinking indicates that people do not have to be tricked or forced to work. In fact, studies show that most people want to do a good job. A majority of workers responded to a recent survey indicating they are not wanted to do all that they could in their job. They wish they could contribute even more!

Getting people motivated is not *making* people do things. It is uncovering the "wanta" factor which is simply learning what they want to do. People get excited about change when they see a part for them in it. They respond with enthusiasm when they feel they have a role in helping define how their work group will be involved in the change. A good leader will offer opportunities for team members to be a part of making change work. This involves asking people for their ideas on how to do it best.

MOTIVATION REQUIRES THOUGHTFUL STRATEGY

INCREASING TEAM INVOLVEMENT
(Continued)

Role of Participation

People will more readily accept change if they are involved in the process. Involvement means that they will have a role in defining how to meet a goal, or respond to a new situation. This is the keynote of participatory management. Participation can take many forms, including:

Quality Circles, Task Forces, Focus Groups, Hot Lines, Opinion Surveys, Suggestion Systems, Brainstorming Meetings, etc.

As a manager you want to use as many of the above options as you can to directly involve your employees in the change process.

Setting the Stage for Involvement

Before beginning to involve your employees in the change process, it is important that you check your intention: Are you involving them because you want to honestly learn how they feel, or are you doing it simply to protect yourself from criticism? Many managers have tried involvement and failed because their intention was to protect themselves, not learn.

Check yourself

Which box describes how you truly feel?

- ☐ Do you think employees need to be watched closely or they will take advantage of the company?
- ☐ Do you think employees are incapable of suggesting the best way to get something done?
- ☐ Do you make certain your employees check with you every step of the way?
- ☐ Do you manage by staying in your office and sending out commands?
- ☐ Do you personally write up employees job descriptions or position statements without consulting them and present them as law?

If you checked any of the above boxes, you need considerable work in learning how to become a participatory manager who trusts employees enough to give them freedom to define their own ways of working.

INCREASING TEAM INVOLVEMENT
(Continued)

Setting Goals Together

You can help your employees through change by insuring you involve them in the setting of goals for their work. Participative goal and objective setting requires open communication in a problem-solving environment. It is a give and take process. A manager who thinks it is his or her sole responsibility to plan, organize, schedule and evaluate work will not be as successful as the one who involves employees in goal-setting. In times of change, goals, and objectives can change frequently and should be re-evaluated often.

Steps for Active Goal Setting During Change

I   **Assess Current Situation**
II   **Listen and Rephrase**
III   **Clarify Objectives**
IV   **Identify Problems**
V   **Brainstorm Solutions**
VI   **Provide Feedback**

Let's consider each step individually:

I. Assess Current Situation—what is happening now?

Does the new work following the change match the current objectives? How have expectations changed since they were last reviewed? Ask open ended questions to find out how each employee feels what is going on relative to new work expectations.

As a manager you may want to become an active listener. Let your employees tell you what is going on. Ask for their ideas on how to best accomplish new responsibilities by asking employees *"If you had to do this how would you go about about it?"*

or,

"If you were the boss and you wanted this to happen how would you go about it?"

You can't make improvements unless you know what is going on.

SETTING GOALS TOGETHER (Continued)

II. Listen and Rephrase—to establish trust

It is impossible to listen and talk at the same time. Listen for the main idea. Take notes to insure you recall what the other person said. Allow enough time for each employee to tell his or her own story completely. Listen for emotion (what are they feeling/experiencing at this time?) Listen with your whole body. Face the employee with uncrossed arms and legs and lean slightly forward. Establish solid, intermittent eye contact. Use affirmative head nods. Occasionally say "uh huh", "go on", "Yes" to encourage the employee. Ask open ended questions (using how, what, where, when, why) and then repeat or restate what you think the other person said. Ask a question to confirm your understanding.

III. Clarify Objectives—what is it that you want and need to achieve?

Work together toward a clear idea of what is wanted. Ask the employee to write out their objectives. Then meet to discuss and revise them. Working together will motivate an employee to do well and will establish a focus for performance.

> **Remember...Objectives are SMART:**
>
> **S**—specific about what is to be accomplished
>
> **M**—measurable
>
> **A**—attainable
>
> **R**—results or output oriented
>
> **T**—time bound

IV. Identify Problems—define and analyze the problems.

In the process of setting goals there will be some areas where you and your employee might not agree. During periods of change it is common to either have too many objectives (the result of combining jobs without cutting out objectives) or trying to do work that fits both the "old" and "new" way of doing things. As a manager, your job is to help prioritize objectives in order to avoid a situation where the employee is overwhelmed. Too many objectives will create anxiety and lead to poor performance.

SETTING GOALS TOGETHER (Continued)

V. Brainstorm Solutions—generate solutions

> During change it's common for jobs to change character. Previous job descriptions are often not accurate and employees may feel upset if they are being asked to do things that are "not their job". To help employees understand their new roles you need to think about:

What has been tried before?

What have other people done in similar situations?

What have you tried before, that may not have worked then, that might work now?

VI. Provide Feedback

> Feedback is essential to employees during change. They need to know how they are doing. They need encouragement and support. Many managers don't do a good job of providing feedback when things are normal.

> Check any reasons you have used for not giving feedback and then vow to change your behavior:

☐ They already know what I think.

☐ I'm the boss, they just need to follow my instructions.

☐ I have too many other things to do.

☐ If anything new happens, I'll tell those who need to know.

☐ They're professionals—they shouldn't need their "hands held."

☐ _____

> When feedback is poor, employees are more likely to be anxious, have low job satisfaction, or quit. People who hear nothing usually fear the worst.

SETTING GOALS TOGETHER (Continued)

How to Improve your Feedback

The purpose of feedback is to help your employees change their behavior in a way it improves their performance. Provide feedback as either information or action. When you provide action oriented feedback, make sure it is something the employee can control. You will only create frustration if you ask them to respond to something they can't do anything about. Following are some tips:

1. Be direct

Give feedback in person. The more people a message goes through, the more likely it is to be distorted. Also, give it as soon as you can.

2. Be specific

People learn from complete information. What behavior, action or style do you want them to continue or discontinue? Simply saying *"Good Job!"* doesn't provide much information. It would be much better to say: *"Thank you for staying late last night to get that shipment out to Mr. Allen. I really appreciate it when you extend yourself."*

3. Be personal

Add yourself to the feedback. Personalize it by putting your feelings in *"I am concerned about your work performance."* or *"I was proud when you were nominated for the safety award"* makes feedback more meaningful. Employees want to hear from **you.**

4. Be honest

Employees can tell when you are faking it. If it isn't honest feedback don't give it at all.

FEEDBACK IS ESSENTIAL FOR SUCCESS

INCREASING TEAM INVOLVEMENT

Reward Attempts, Not Just Achievements

There will be mistakes made during changes. How you respond to them will be important in maintaining employee involvement. Each mistake represents a potential for learning. It is your job to focus employees on the learning aspect of the mistake. Ask what they will do in the future to prevent the mistake from happening again. Provide positive reinforcement to their ideas and give them your support to try again.

One way to reduce damage from mistakes is to have regular cycles of report and feedback. This is especially important during changes when the pre-established ways of working are often off the mark.

How Performance is Affected Through Change

Change in the workplace will affect your employee's job performance. Performance will usually be affected in direct proportion to the magnitude of the change. If the change is significant it is safe to assume that job activities will not be accomplished at a normal rate. Factor this slow down in your production expectations and scheduling.

Before, during and after change there are specific things employees want from their jobs. Make sure you provide as many of the following as possible:

1. Work that is interesting and/or meaningful.
2. Clear statement of the results you expect.
3. Appropriate and on-time feedback on those results.
4. A reward system for achieving results.

During change you have an excellent opportunity to re-think job descriptions and assignments to make them more meaningful. Job enrichment can be nothing more than taking a current job and involving the employee to make it more meaningful. This may involve adding responsibilities, varying or rotating tasks, or getting the job done in new ways.

Describe a job in your work group that may be a candidate for enrichment.

_____

_____

RE-DEFINING A JOB

Use the following steps to job enrichment in re-defining jobs during change. You have permission to make copies of this form for all jobs you wish to re-define.

Analyze how a job is presently done.

1. Procedures

_____

_____

_____

2. Tools/Techniques/Skills required

_____

_____

_____

3. Scope of Authority. Who supervises? What is their authority?

_____

_____

_____

4. Schedule for Completing Work

_____

_____

_____

5. Interpersonal Relationship—who does the employee interact with?

_____

_____

_____

6. Anything else that is essential

_____

_____

_____

RE-DEFINING A JOB (Continued)

Look at the information you gathered on page 59 and re-think each job using the
following principles:

1. What is the overall mission/direction/meaning of the job? Is the job a consistant
unit, not just stray pieces?

_____

_____

_____

_____

_____

2. How can you communicate to the employee that the job makes a contribution?
What are the markers of individual accountability?

_____

_____

_____

_____

_____

3. How can the employee participate in the planning of the work to be performed?

_____

_____

_____

_____

_____

SECTION VII

VISIONARY LEADERSHIP

"Leadership is more tribal than scientific, more a weaving of relationships than amassing information. . ."

Max DuPree *Leadership is an Art*

BECOMING A LEADER DURING CHANGE

Being a leader during change is not easy. Different management skills are needed. Less hands on control and more "framing" and "bridging" occurs. The span of control often increases and managers may be responsible for more people and different challenges. To succeed, an energized leader will do more to focus the efforts of his or her employees. This requires

- Understanding and articulating a vision of where the group is going.
- Sharing that vision
- Creating an environment where employees feel a sense of making the vision come true.

Many managers say they feel powerless in their role during change, being squeezed between pressures from above and below. In this section you will learn some tools you can use to lead your group into the future. They do not require top management's approval to implement. Remember what was said earlier—i.e., if you are waiting for your company to tell you how to change before you lead your group through the change, you may be waiting for a very long time.

STEP 1
Creating a vision with your group

When change occurs we have to move from "how it was" to a vision of "how it will be." After a group has progressed beyond denial and resistance, it is common to experience a surge in energy. People start preparing themselves to face the future. They explore where they stand, new results that need to be achieved, and what opportunities lie ahead. At this stage, they need to help to create a vision of their goal. To help this happen you can lead your group toward a shared vision of the future. Many of the extraordinary things ordinary people achieve, begin with a vision that inspires and empowers them. During transition, a change leader will help his or her group set a clear direction of where the team needs to head.

BECOMING A LEADER DURING CHANGE
(Continued)

STEP 2
Team Visioning

Set some time aside to discuss the future. Schedule a special meeting to focus on the future.

Ask your team to close their eyes and imagine themselves five years in the future. The organization's major transistion is over. Ask them what they notice in their workplace of the future? What is the organization like? What are people doing? What are work areas like? What type work is being done? As they explore their workplace of the future, ask them to think about how the future is different from today. What improvements do they notice?

Next, hold a discussion about what people noticed. Write key points of their visions on a flip-chart. From what was volunteered, create a shared vision of the future.

OUR VISION OF THE FUTURE IS:

Working on a vision can be an exciting process. It can help employees realize they play a part in shaping their future. Instead of worrying about an uncertain future, visioning can help a team generate a shared sense of where they are headed. From the vision you create, it is possible to work backwards to design ways to reach this vision.

STEP 3
Clarifying values

Change can lead to a re-configuration of the values your team operates by. Values are the foundation for the way you work together. During change, basic values may shift. For example, a company that once valued strict procedures and tradition, may shift toward valuing independence and new markets. One thing you can do is clarify what the previous values have been and what the new values will be.

WORK VALUES EXERCISE

A **value** is a principle or standard that you consider worthwhile and that you use to live or work by. The following values are common in a work environment. How important is each member of your team? Make a copy of this form and invite your work group to individually complete this exercise.

	Least Important				Most Important
Security—freedom from worry, safety, certainty, predictability	1	2	3	4	5
Status—how you appear in the eyes of others	1	2	3	4	5
Compensation—pay or remuneration	1	2	3	4	5
Advancement—improvement, progress	1	2	3	4	5
Affiliation—being associated with and liked by co-workers	1	2	3	4	5
Recognition—getting noticed for individual or team effort	1	2	3	4	5
Authority—having the power to direct events	1	2	3	4	5
Achievement—mastery of task, project or skills to get job done	1	2	3	4	5
Independence—freedom from control of others	1	2	3	4	5
Altruism—concern for the well-being of others	1	2	3	4	5
Creativity—finding new ways to do things, being innovative	1	2	3	4	5
Intellectual Stimulation—critical thinking, new ideas	1	2	3	4	5
Asthetic—desire for beauty in work and surroundings	1	2	3	4	5
(Other important values to your group)					
_____	1	2	3	4	5
_____	1	2	3	4	5
_____	1	2	3	4	5

After each team member has clarified personal values, lead your team in a discussion about your group's shared values and attempt to come up with the primary work values reflected by your team.

The main values of our work group include:

_____

_____

_____

WORK VALUES EXERCISE (Continued)

Keep the discussion of values concrete. Don't let people talk abstractly. Give specific examples of how you would know you were acting according to these values.

For example, commitment might be expressed by our being responsible for getting substitutes when we must stay home from work.

Don't be afraid to talk openly about desired values that may be obscured or forgotten due to business pressures.

Values are the new glue

Shared values allow you to work together using a balance of delegation and control. During change you will probably find your culture is growing to include a wider range of values. This is normal. Traditional work cultures were often narrowly defined and demanded a high degree of conformity. There was a "right" way to do things and if you wanted to belong, you did those things. Today, with cultures in flux, there is a wider range of "what is right", more room for creativity, individual initiative and change. The new work group operates not according to tradition, but using vision and shared values. Team members in the future will have to make more independent decisions. Your job as a team leader is to keep them enthused and directed toward the targets they have set.

Finding the New Way

After a team has clarified its vision and values, your task as a change leader is to help your team explore how they can best accomplish their goals. Once this has occured it will be possible to choose and commit to a plan of action.

SETTING A PLAN OF ACTION

An action plan can be accomplished in a brainstorming meeting, or series of meetings, where employees feel welcome to suggest ideas about how to accomplish goals based on the group's shared vision. Sometimes, when a new technology or significantly different organization is initiated, many corresponding changes may be required.

Exploration is a period of time where your team makes an extra effort to think about new ways of doing things. A team, when working well, can often think of more and better ways to achieve results. Draw on the energy of the group to think about how to make positive things happen.

Planning sessions may seem to be inefficient. But you will find planning well worth the time. People want to participate and become involved. Often they will spend time on their own resolving specific challenges.

After a period of brainstorming, you should lead your group to some decisions. This means setting specific goals and obtaining agreement on a plan to meet them. Making decisions as a team helps everyone commit to them.

Once you have committed to new goals, you should take time to recognize contributions each individual has made.

SECTION VIII
CHANGE ACTION PLAN

The only things that evolve by themselves in an organization are disorder, friction and malperformance.

Peter Drucker

AN ACTION PLAN FOR SUCCESS

It's now time to put all that you have learned together, and create an **Action Plan** for responding to change in your workplace. Take time to answer each of the questions below, for changes that you face:

1. Describe the change as completely as you can. State specifically how it will impact your employees, department and organization. Note ''human factors'' that will be affected by the change.

   _____

   _____

   _____

   _____

2. What is your vision of the best possible outcome?

   _____

   _____

   _____

   _____

3. What are the strengths of your group/department in undertaking this change?

   _____

   _____

   _____

   _____

4. What are the obstacles the change will bring to prevent you from reaching your goal?

   _____

   _____

   _____

   _____

AN ACTION PLAN FOR SUCCESS (Continued)

5. List the Action Steps for:

Communication _____

_____

_____

Dealing with Resistance _____

_____

_____

Involvement _____

_____

_____

Leadership _____

_____

_____

6. What is your timetable for making this change?

Now _____

_____

_____

_____ Finish

7. What new skills, knowledge and attitudes are needed to make this change?

Skills _____

_____

_____

Knowledge _____

_____

_____

Attitudes _____

_____

AN ACTION PLAN FOR SUCCESS (Continued)

8. How will you acknowledge, recognize and celebrate this change?

    _____

    _____

    _____

    _____

9. How will you create incentives to move toward change?

    _____

    _____

    _____

    _____

10. How will you reward yourselves for having led this change?

    _____

    _____

    _____

    _____

RECOMMENDED READING

Adams, John, ed. *Transforming Leadership*. Alexandria, Virginia: Miles River Press 1986.

Bennis, Warren & Nanus, Bert. *Leaders*. New York: Harper and Row, 1985.

Bridges, William. *Surviving Corporate Transitions*. New York: Doubleday, 1988.

Deal, Terrence, and Kennedy, William. *Corporate Cultures*. Reading, Massachusetts: Addison-Wesley, 1982.

Hirschhorn, Larry and Associates. *Cutting Back*. San Francisco, California: Jossey Bass, 1983.

Kanter, Rosabeth Moss. *The Change Masters*. New York, Simon and Schuster, 1983.

Kilmann, Ralph. *Beyond the Quick Fix*. San Francisco, California: Jossey-Bass, 1984.

Levering, Robert. *A Great Place to Work*. New York: Random House, 1988.

Michaels, Donald. *Learning to Plan, Planning to Learn*. San Francisco, California: Jossey-Bass, 1973.

Miller, William. *The Creative Edge*. Reading, Massachusetts: Addison-Wesley, 1987.

Morgan, Gareth. *Riding the Waves of Change*. San Francisco, California: Jossey-Bass, 1988.

O'Toole, James. *Vanguard Leadership*. New York: Doubleday, 1985.

Pinchot, Gifford. *Intrapreneuring*. New York: Harper and Row, 1985.

Peters, Tom. *Thriving on Chaos*. New York, Alfred A. Knopf, 1988.

Theobold, Robert. *The Rapids of Change*. Knowledge Press, 1988.

Tichy, Noel and Mary Ann Devanna. *The Transformational Manager*. New York: John Wiley, 1987.

Torbert, William. *Managing the Corporate Dream*. New York: Dow Jones Irwin, 1986.

Waterman, Robert. *The Renewal Factor*. New York: Bantam, 1988.

Woodward, Harry & Steve Buchholz. *Aftershock*. New York: John Wiley, 1987.

RECOMMENDED READING

NOTES

FOR OTHER FIFTY-MINUTE SELF-STUDY BOOKS
SEE ORDER FORM AT THE BACK OF THE BOOK.

NOTES

FOR OTHER FIFTY-MINUTE SELF-STUDY BOOKS
SEE ORDER FORM AT THE BACK OF THE BOOK.

NOTES

FOR OTHER FIFTY-MINUTE SELF-STUDY BOOKS
SEE ORDER FORM AT THE BACK OF THE BOOK.

NOTES

FOR OTHER FIFTY-MINUTE SELF-STUDY BOOKS
SEE ORDER FORM AT THE BACK OF THE BOOK.

ABOUT THE FIFTY-MINUTE SERIES

"Every so often an idea emerges that is so simple and appealing, people wonder why it didn't come along sooner. The Fifty-Minute series is just such an idea. Excellent!"

Mahaliah Levine, Vice President for
Training and Development
Dean Witter Reynolds, Inc.

WHAT IS A FIFTY-MINUTE BOOK?

—Fifty-Minute books are brief, soft-covered, "self-study" titles covering a wide variety of topics pertaining to business and self-improvement. They are reasonably priced, ideal for formal training, excellent for self-study and perfect for remote location training.

"A Fifty-Minute book gives the reader fundamentals that can be applied on the job, even before attending a formal class"

Lynn Baker, Manager of Training
Fleming Corporation

WHY ARE FIFTY-MINUTE BOOKS UNIQUE?

—Because of their format. Designed to be "read with a pencil," the basics of a subject can be quickly grasped and applied through a series of hands-on activities, exercises and cases.

"Fifty-Minute books are the best new publishing idea in years. They are clear, practical, concise and affordable—perfect for today's world."

Leo Hauser, Past President
ASTD

HOW MANY FIFTY-MINUTE BOOKS ARE THERE?

—Those listed on the following pages at this time. Additional titles are always in development. For more information write to **Crisp Publications, Inc.,**
95 First Street, Los Altos, CA 94022.

THE FIFTY-MINUTE SERIES

Quantity	Title	Code #	Price	Amount
	MANAGEMENT TRAINING			
	Successful Negotiation	09-2	$7.95	
	Personal Performance Contracts	12-2	$7.95	
	Team Building	16-5	$7.95	
	Effective Meeting Skills	33-5	$7.95	
	An Honest Day's Work	39-4	$7.95	
	Managing Disagreement Constructively	41-6	$7.95	
	Training Managers To Train	43-2	$7.95	
	The Fifty-Minute Supervisor	58-0	$7.95	
	Leadership Skills For Women	62-9	$7.95	
	Problem Solving & Decision Making	63-7	$7.95	
	Coaching & Counseling For Supervisors	68-8	$7.95	
	Management Dilemmas: A Guide to Business Ethics	69-6	$7.95	
	Understanding Organizational Change	71-8	$7.95	
	Project Management	75-0	$7.95	
	Managing Organizational Change	80-7	$7.95	
	Managing A Diverse Workforce	85-8	$7.95	
	PERSONNEL TRAINING & HUMAN RESOURCE MANAGEMENT			
	Effective Performance Appraisals	11-4	$7.95	
	Quality Interviewing	13-0	$7.95	
	Personal Counseling	14-9	$7.95	
	Job Performance and Chemical Dependency	27-0	$7.95	
	New Employee Orientation	46-7	$7.95	
	Professional Excellence for Secretaries	52-1	$7.95	
	Guide To Affirmative Action	54-8	$7.95	
	Writing A Human Resource Manual	70-X	$7.95	
	COMMUNICATIONS			
	Effective Presentation Skills	24-6	$7.95	
	Better Business Writing	25-4	$7.95	
	The Business of Listening	34-3	$7.95	
	Writing Fitness	35-1	$7.95	
	The Art of Communicating	45-9	$7.95	
	Technical Presentation Skills	55-6	$7.95	
	Making Humor Work	61-0	$7.95	
	Better Technical Writing	64-5	$7.95	
	Influencing Others: A Practical Guide	84-X	$7.95	
	Using Visual Aids in Business	89-0	$7.95	
	SELF-MANAGEMENT			
	Balancing Home And Career	10-6	$7.95	
	Mental Fitness: A Guide to Emotional Health	15-7	$7.95	
	Personal Financial Fitness	20-3	$7.95	
	Attitude: Your Most Priceless Possession	21-1	$7.95	
	Personal Time Management	22-X	$7.95	

(Continued on next page)

THE FIFTY-MINUTE SERIES

Quantity	Title	Code #	Price	Amount
	SELF-MANAGEMENT (CONTINUED)			
	Preventing Job Burnout	23-8	$7.95	
	Successful Self-Management	26-2	$7.95	
	Developing Positive Assertiveness	38-6	$7.95	
	Time Management And The Telephone	53-X	$7.95	
	Memory Skills In Business	56-4	$7.95	
	Developing Self-Esteem	66-1	$7.95	
	Creativity In Business	67-X	$7.95	
	Quality At Work	72-6	$7.95	
	Managing Personal Change	74-2	$7.95	
	Speedreading For Better Productivity	78-5	$7.95	
	Winning At Human Relations	86-6	$7.95	
	Stop Procrastinating	88-2	$7.95	
	SALES TRAINING/QUALITY CUSTOMER SERVICE			
	Sales Training Basics	02-5	$7.95	
	Restaurant Server's Guide	08-4	$7.95	
	Quality Customer Service	17-3	$7.95	
	Telephone Courtesy And Customer Service	18-1	$7.95	
	Professional Selling	42-4	$7.95	
	Customer Satisfaction	57-2	$7.95	
	Telemarketing Basics	60-2	$7.95	
	Calming Upset Customers	65-3	$7.95	
	Managing A Quality Service Organization	83-1	$7.95	
	ENTREPRENEURSHIP			
	Marketing Your Consulting Or Professional Services	40-8	$7.95	
	Starting Your Small Business	44-0	$7.95	
	Publicity Power	82-3	$7.95	
	CAREER GUIDANCE & STUDY SKILLS			
	Study Skills Strategies	05-X	$7.95	
	Career Discovery	07-6	$7.95	
	Plan B: Protecting Your Career From The Winds of Change	48-3	$7.95	
	I Got The Job!	59-9	$7.95	
	OTHER CRISP INC. BOOKS			
	Comfort Zones: A Practical Guide For Retirement Planning	00-9	$13.95	
	Stepping Up To Supervisor	11-8	$13.95	
	The Unfinished Business Of Living: Helping Aging Parents	19-X	$12.95	
	Managing Performance	23-7	$18.95	
	Be True To Your Future: A Guide to Life Planning	47-5	$13.95	
	Up Your Productivity	49-1	$10.95	
	How To Succeed In A Man's World	79-3	$7.95	
	Practical Time Management	275-4	$13.95	
	Copyediting: A Practical Guide	51-3	$18.95	

THE FIFTY-MINUTE SERIES
(Continued)

☐ Send volume discount information.

☐ Please send me a catalog.

	Amount
Total (from other side)	
Shipping ($1.50 first book, $.50 per title thereafter)	
California Residents add 7% tax	
Total	

Ship to: _____

_____

_____

_____

Phone number: _____

Bill to: _____

_____

_____

_____

P.O. # _____

**All orders except those with a P.O.# must be prepaid.
For more information Call (415) 949-4888 or FAX (415) 949-1610.**

BUSINESS REPLY
FIRST CLASS   PERMIT NO. 884   LOS ALTOS, CA

POSTAGE WILL BE PAID BY ADDRESSEE

Crisp Publications, Inc.
95 First Street
Los Altos, CA 94022

NO POSTAGE
NECESSARY
IF MAILED
IN THE
UNITED STATES